MY MOMMY IS
AN UNDERCOVER SPY

WRITTEN BY **BRITNEY PICKETT** & **JOHN PICKETT**
ILLUSTRATED BY **MARTÍN QUERIO**
A PBNJ WAY PRODUCTION

the PBNJ way PRODUCTION

MY MOMMY IS AN UNDERCOVER SPY

WRITTEN BY **BRITNEY PICKETT & JOHN PICKETT**

ILLUSTRATED BY **MARTÍN QUERIO**

We dedicate this work of art to our three beautiful children who get to grow up with a working mommy who loves them more than words could ever express.

To Mom, I could never have made it here without the hardest working and compassionate person ever helping me through it all. You are a real life super hero.

SHE IS MORE

THAN JUST MY MOMMY

Mommy drinks a steaming cup of secret serum every morning. She calls it coffee. This hot cup of serum is off limits to me. She only makes it when everyone is sleeping, so I've never seen the ingredients. She drinks it from the same mug every day even though we have a million other cups. I'm sure this one must hold all the power.

It's always too hot for me to hold. She does this on purpose to prevent me from inhaling the potent fumes. Mommy says I can't have any serum because coffee is not for kids. I don't argue because even I know that a boiling secret serum that mists magical potion, is off limits to plain ole regular people.

CLUE #4

Mommy leaves the house for *very long* periods of time. An extraordinarily large amount of time goes by when we do not see each other. So long, that I only see her when it is completely dark outside. This is totally by her design. If it is only dark when I see her, I can't search for evidence to support my theory in her transformer briefcase or password protected computer.

MOMMY LEAVES THE HOUSE FOR

I would never be able to get in anyway, her gizmo gadgets only open for her. If my mommy is not a spy, why does her cellular device require facial recognition to open?

VERY LONG
PERIODS OF TIME

Mommy avoids long telephone conversations. This is how she stops anyone from listening to her phone calls and getting access to her master plans. She wont even pick up her cell phone but she will answer her office phone. Daddy calls it a landline. She does this to stop interception of her messages and protect her operation.

She is always putting the phone on silent at random times and whispering like she doesn't want to blow her cover. I even overheard her mentioning expiring deadlines as she was sneaking into a vacant room and locking the door. Who was she trying to escape from?

CLUE #6

Mommy has a secret home office just for herself. She keeps written notes with scribbly writing attached to every surface of it. I know spy code when I see it. Some have numbers, others with graphs, and a few with charts. When I stare hard enough, I can begin to decode the messages. She is preparing for her next mission!

There are wild stacks of papers and computer screens everywhere. How much intel does one spy need to do? I sneak into the room every chance I get to see where she is going next, and she always knows I'm in there. Clever, mommy set up invisible sensors to keep me out of current events just in case she gets caught.

What's most amazing, is when mommy is done sneaking into booby trapped buildings and saving the world, she makes time to be with me. ME! Out of all the people a seasoned secret spy could spend time with! Mommy says it's important for us to read together, eat together, play together, and give big hugs every single day. This is the *best* time of my day but I know that only a spy could pull off this double life.

If I wasn't paying such close attention, she would be successful in hiding her *real* job, with her heartfelt hugs, warm kisses, and beloved bedtime stories. Mommy doesn't fool me.

So here's a word of caution to all my kid friends out there: If any of this behavior sounds familiar,

BEWARE YOUR MOMMY - MAY BE AN AMAZINGLY AGILE, EFFORTLESSLY EDGY, PARTICULARLY POWERFUL, UNDERCOVER SPY, JUST LIKE MINE.

TO ALL THE WORKING MOMMIES IN THE WORLD, YOU'RE DOING GREAT! YOUR YEARS OF EARLY MORNINGS AND LATE NIGHTS ARE GREATLY APPRECIATED. YOUR CHILDREN GET THE PROVILEDGE TO GROW UP WATCHING MOMMY TAKE OVER HER WORLD ONE DAY AT A TIME.